Chapter 1: Understanding AI

What is AI?

In its most basic form, AI, or *Artificial Intelligence*, is a field of computer science dedicated to creating systems capable of performing tasks that, until recently, required human intelligence. These tasks include things like understanding natural language, recognizing patterns, solving problems, and making decisions.

The term 'Artificial Intelligence' was first coined by John McCarthy in 1956, who defined it as "the science and engineering of making intelligent machines." In other words, the goal of AI is to create machines that can function intelligently and independently.

But what does it mean for a machine to be 'intelligent'?

In the context of AI, intelligence is typically understood as the ability to learn from experience, adapt to new situations, understand complex concepts, and employ these understandings to manipulate the environment or achieve certain goals. When a machine possesses these abilities, it is considered 'intelligent.'

AI can be divided into two primary types: *Narrow AI and General AI.*

Narrow AI, also known as Weak AI, is designed to perform a single task, such as voice recognition. These systems operate under a limited set of constraints and are designed to do one thing very well. Examples of Narrow AI that we encounter in our daily lives include recommendation systems like those used by Amazon or Netflix, voice assistants such as Siri or Alexa, and self-driving car technology.

On the other hand, General AI, also referred to as Strong AI, is a type of AI that has the potential to understand, learn, and apply knowledge across a wide range of tasks at a level equal to or beyond a human being. As of now, General AI remains largely theoretical, with no existing systems possessing the wide-ranging and adaptable intelligence that this term implies.

Understanding the distinction between these types of AI is essential, as it not only provides us with a clearer view of the current capabilities and limitations of AI technology but also helps to demystify some of the fear and uncertainty surrounding this rapidly evolving field.

Brief History of AI

The history of Artificial Intelligence (AI) is as captivating as the technology itself. It's a story filled with peaks and troughs, where periods of excitement and rapid advancement are followed by "AI winters" characterized by reduced interest and funding.

The concept of AI, in its earliest form, can be traced back to ancient civilizations, with myths, stories, and speculation about artificial beings endowed with intelligence or consciousness by master craftsmen; Greek myths of automated servants like Hephaestus's golden robots can be considered an ancient precursor to the concept of AI.

But the real inception of AI as we know it today took place in the 20th century. The term 'Artificial Intelligence' was coined in 1956 by John McCarthy at the Dartmouth Conference, where the core mission of AI — creating a machine capable of simulating every aspect of human intelligence — was established.

In the early years, AI researchers were optimistic. They made predictions about machines being capable of doing any work a human can do within a few decades. They developed early AI programs that demonstrated problem-solving ability, knowledge, learning, and even language understanding.

However, as the field progressed, researchers realized that creating intelligent machines was more difficult than they'd anticipated. The problem was that these early systems lacked the ability to 'understand' the tasks they performed; they followed rules without understanding their underlying meaning. This led to the first 'AI winter' in the mid-1970s, a period of disappointment and funding cuts due to unmet expectations.

AI made a resurgence in the 1980s with the advent of expert systems, which simulated the knowledge and analytical skills of human experts. However, the high costs and maintenance needs led to another downturn by the end of the decade.

The 1990s and early 2000s saw significant advancements in technology, including machine learning, intelligent tutoring, data mining, and more. AI slowly began to become part of everyday life, appearing in products like speech recognition systems and recommendation engines.

The breakthrough moment for AI came with the advent of deep learning and neural networks in the 2010s. These technologies allow AI systems to learn directly from large amounts of data, leading to massive advancements in image and speech recognition, language processing, and other AI applications.

Today, AI is in a period of rapid growth and development, with increasing interest and investment from both the public and private sectors. It's being applied in a variety of fields, from healthcare and education to transportation and entertainment, making it a truly integral part of our modern world.

While AI has come a long way since its inception, it's important to remember that we are still in the early stages of this technology. As we continue to explore and advance the capabilities of AI, the possibilities for the future are virtually limitless.

Different types of AI

As we delve deeper into the world of Artificial Intelligence, it's crucial to understand that AI is not a monolithic entity, but rather a broad field encompassing various sub-disciplines. Let's explore some of the major types of AI: Machine Learning, Deep Learning, and Neural Networks.

Machine Learning

At its core, Machine Learning (ML) is a type of AI that provides systems the ability to learn and improve from experience without being explicitly programmed. The idea is to develop algorithms that can receive input data and use statistical analysis to predict an output while updating outputs as new data becomes available.

Machine Learning is further categorized into three types: Supervised Learning, where the model learns from labeled data; Unsupervised Learning, where the model learns from unlabeled data and finds patterns within; and Reinforcement Learning, where an agent learns to behave in an environment by performing certain actions and receiving rewards.

Deep Learning

Deep Learning is a subset of Machine Learning, inspired by the structure and function of the human brain, specifically the interconnections among neurons. It uses artificial neural networks with several layers - hence the 'deep' in Deep Learning. These layered neural networks can learn and make intelligent decisions on their own.

Deep Learning algorithms automatically learn the optimal features for a task, given enough computational resources and data. This ability makes them highly effective and versatile, contributing to their use in image and speech recognition, natural language processing, and more.

Neural Networks

Neural Networks, or Artificial Neural Networks (ANNs), serve as the backbone of Deep Learning. They're designed to replicate the way human brain's function, using interconnected layers of nodes ('artificial neurons') to process and transmit information.

A Neural Network takes in inputs, which are processed in hidden layers using weights that are adjusted during training. The model then provides an output. This output is then compared with the desired output, and the weights are adjusted to get closer to the correct result.

A specific type of neural network that has revolutionized AI is the Convolutional Neural Network (CNN). These networks are especially good at processing grid-like data, such as images, making them instrumental in the field of computer vision.

While Machine Learning, Deep Learning, and Neural Networks are critical pieces of the AI puzzle, it's worth mentioning that there are other types of AI, such as Natural Language Processing (NLP), Robotics, and Expert Systems. Each type serves a different purpose and uses unique techniques, contributing to the vast and complex world of AI.

As we move forward in our exploration of AI, it's crucial to understand these key concepts. While they may seem intimidating at first, each plays a pivotal role in harnessing the full potential of AI and offers a glimpse into the future of this transformative technology.

Chapter 2: Common Misconceptions about AI

As with any transformative technology, artificial intelligence has been met with a degree of fear and uncertainty. These fears, often fueled by sensationalized media portrayals and a lack of clear understanding, lead to misconceptions that can hinder the acceptance and progression of AI. Let's address some of the most common fears and misconceptions.

Common Fear: *AI Will Replace All Human Jobs*
One of the most common fears is that AI will automate jobs to the point where human workers become obsolete. It's true that AI and automation will change the way we work, and some jobs may be phased out. However, history has shown that while technology can eliminate

certain jobs, it also creates new ones. Furthermore, AI is more likely to automate tasks, not entire jobs, allowing human workers to focus more on complex, creative, and interpersonal aspects of their work.

Common Misconception: AI is Infallible
AI can process vast amounts of information and perform complex calculations at incredible speeds, leading some to believe that AI is infallible. However, AI is far from perfect. AI algorithms are created by humans, which means they can inherit our biases and make mistakes, especially when they encounter situations outside their training data. The belief in AI's infallibility can lead to overreliance on AI systems, underscoring the importance of human oversight and understanding.

Common Fear: AI Can Turn Against Us
Popular culture is rife with stories of AI systems becoming sentient and turning against their human creators. However, current AI technology is far from achieving the level of consciousness or understanding required for such a scenario. Today's AI operates within a narrow set of parameters and is not capable of any desires or motivations.

Common Misconception: AI Understands Like Humans Do
While AI can mimic human-like tasks, like understanding speech or identifying images, it doesn't 'understand' these tasks in the way humans do. AI lacks the ability to conceptualize or contextualize information. For example, an AI can identify a cat in an image because it's learned the patterns in the data, not because it fully understands what a cat is.

Common Fear: AI Will Lead to a Loss of Privacy
With AI's ability to analyze and make decisions based on vast amounts of data, there is a legitimate fear about privacy. While this concern is valid, it's important to remember that the use of AI in data processing doesn't inherently lead to privacy violations. The key lies in strong regulations and ethical guidelines to ensure that AI technology respects user privacy.

Where do these Misconceptions Stem From?

Complexity and Lack of Understanding

Artificial Intelligence is a marvel of modern technology. It powers innovations that seemed like science fiction just a few decades ago — from self-driving cars to virtual assistants and powerful diagnostic tools in healthcare. Yet, for all its wonders, the inner workings of AI are often shrouded in mystery. Its complexity and the lack of widespread understanding can fuel misconceptions, leading to misplaced fears or unrealistic expectations.

At the heart of AI are algorithms, neural networks, and machine learning, the intricate concepts that even tech-savvy individuals may struggle to fully grasp. Algorithms are like recipes, providing step-by-step instructions for how an AI system should perform a task. Neural networks, inspired by the human brain, consist of interconnected layers of nodes or 'neurons' that work together to process information and generate outputs. Machine learning, a subset of AI, involves systems learning from data, improving their performance without explicit programming.

These concepts, although straightforward in their essence, quickly become complex when delved into. The depth and breadth of the mathematical and computational knowledge required to understand AI in detail are beyond the reach of the average person. As a result, most people have a superficial understanding of AI, which often leads to the development of simplified, and frequently erroneous, mental models of how AI operates.

One common misconception is *anthropomorphism* — attributing human-like qualities, capabilities, or intentions to AI. While it's true that some AI systems can mimic human behavior or learn from experiences, they don't possess consciousness, emotions, or desires. AI systems do what they are programmed to do, nothing more, nothing less. Yet, people often ascribe them a level of autonomy and understanding that they simply don't have.

On the other end of the spectrum, the complexity of AI can lead to an underestimation of its capabilities. Some might dismiss AI as a mere buzzword or fail to recognize the advanced computational tasks it can perform. This underestimation could cause individuals and businesses to miss out on the benefits of implementing AI solutions or fall behind in the rapidly advancing technological landscape.

Addressing these misunderstandings is vital. A more informed public can lead to more nuanced discussions about AI's implications and a better collective decision-making process about its deployment and regulation. As we continue to interact with AI more frequently in our daily lives, it's important for everyone to have at least a basic understanding of what AI is, what it can do, and what it can't do.

Education plays a crucial role in this process. It starts with initiatives at all levels — from schools incorporating basics of AI in their curriculum, to businesses training their staff about AI applications relevant to their work, to media outlets reporting about AI in a more accurate and responsible manner.

A clearer understanding of AI can help us make the most of its potential while minimizing the risks associated with its misuse or misunderstanding. After all, fear often stems from the unknown — the more we understand AI, the less we have to fear.

Media and Popular Culture Influence

Media and popular culture wield a powerful influence over public perceptions of Artificial Intelligence. Movies, TV shows, books, and even news outlets can significantly shape how we perceive and understand AI. This influence, however, is a double-edged sword. While these platforms can enlighten and inform, they can also propagate misconceptions and fears about AI that are far from the current reality of the technology.

Science fiction has long been fascinated with the concept of AI. From sentient machines rising against humanity in "The Terminator" and "The Matrix," to advanced AI systems flawlessly running entire spaceships in "Star Trek" or "2001: A Space Odyssey," AI in popular culture is often depicted at the extreme ends of the spectrum. It's either portrayed as an existential threat or as an infallible technology that has achieved perfection.

These portrayals can be highly entertaining and thought-provoking, but they also contribute to a skewed perception of what AI is and what it can do. The sentient, rogue AI systems seen on screen bear little resemblance to the AI technology of today, which is more about recognizing patterns in data, translating languages, recommending products, and playing complex board games than about taking over the world or achieving consciousness.

Likewise, the image of AI as an infallible solution to every problem is far from reality. While AI can be powerful and efficient, it is not without its limitations. AI systems are as good as the data they're trained on and the algorithms that power them. They can make mistakes, and they don't possess the common sense, creativity, or emotional understanding of a human being.

Even news media can contribute to AI misconceptions. Sensationalist headlines or stories may overstate AI capabilities or threats for the sake of more clicks and shares. Such reporting can lead to overblown fears or unrealistic expectations among the public.

To foster a more accurate understanding of AI, it's important to separate the fascinating world of science fiction from the realities of AI technology. Educators, researchers, journalists, and technology leaders all have a role to play in this. They need to present a balanced view of AI, one that highlights its potential benefits and achievements, but also acknowledges its limitations and the challenges that come with its implementation.

This doesn't mean we should stop enjoying AI's portrayal in popular culture. These stories often reflect our hopes, fears, and ethical dilemmas concerning AI and can spark valuable discussions. However, they should be taken for what they are - entertaining and thought-provoking fiction, not accurate depictions of current or near-future AI technology.

In our journey towards understanding and embracing AI, it's vital to seek out reliable and balanced sources of information and not to let sensationalist media or dramatic science fiction shape our perception of this powerful technology. The more we understand the realities of AI, the more we can separate the fear from the fascination.

Anthropomorphism

Anthropomorphism—the attribution of human characteristics or behaviors to non-human entities—is a tendency deeply rooted in the human psyche. From ancient times, when our ancestors imbued natural phenomena with human qualities, to today's era of advanced AI, we find comfort and familiarity in humanizing the non-human. However, when it comes to understanding Artificial Intelligence, anthropomorphism can lead to significant misconceptions.

This phenomenon manifests prominently when we interact with voice-based AI assistants like Siri or Alexa. These systems are designed to understand our speech and respond in kind, often with colloquialisms and elements of humor that make the interaction feel more human-like. Such nuances can leave us with the impression that we're communicating with a conscious entity that understands and reciprocates our feelings.

However, beneath their sophisticated exteriors, these AI assistants are not sentient. They don't understand or experience emotions. Instead, they rely on complex algorithms and extensive databases to interpret our queries and generate relevant responses. The feeling of conversing with a 'thinking' entity is an illusion crafted by clever programming and our own anthropomorphic tendencies.

Similarly, anthropomorphism comes into play in the field of robotics. Robots, such as Boston Dynamics' Spot or SoftBank's Pepper, often feature humanoid or animal-like designs to foster relatability and engagement. Witnessing these robots move or interact with their environment in seemingly 'intelligent' ways can make us perceive them as conscious beings with individual intent. However, despite their lifelike behaviors, these robots are but machines, responding according to their programming and controls—they don't possess consciousness or free will.

Our inclination to anthropomorphize AI can blur our understanding of its capabilities and limitations. By imagining AI as human-like, we risk both overestimating its abilities and underestimating its constraints. We might believe that AI systems understand, care, or function autonomously, when in fact they are executing human-designed responses devoid of comprehension or emotion.

It's crucial, then, to recognize our propensity for anthropomorphism in our encounters with AI. While it's natural to humanize these systems due to their sophisticated behaviors, we must remember that they lack human consciousness or emotions. Their actions, no matter how complex or human-like, are ultimately determined by human-created programming and control. By maintaining this awareness, we can foster a more accurate and realistic understanding of Artificial Intelligence, enabling us to harness its potential responsibly and effectively.

Human Nature: Fear of Change and the Unknown

The fear of change and the unknown is a deeply ingrained human instinct that surfaces when we encounter significant transformations—especially when these transformations are driven by emerging technologies. AI, with its profound potential to disrupt the status quo, is no exception. It has, quite naturally, become a source of apprehension, fostering resistance in some quarters. Much of this fear is intertwined with the essence of AI: its complexity, its vast capabilities, and the element of uncertainty surrounding its future applications and implications.

A parallel can be drawn to the late 1990s, when the internet was steadily making its way into mainstream society, promising to alter every aspect of our lives. This era, often referred to as the "Dot-com Bubble," was characterized by a mix of excitement and fear. The internet—much like AI today—represented an unknown territory, triggering widespread apprehension.

Many feared that the advent of e-commerce would spell the end for traditional brick-and-mortar stores. There were also concerns about privacy, with the internet enabling easy access to personal information, and worries about job displacement as new digital skills became necessary.

Interestingly, looking back, we find that the fears, while not entirely baseless, were often overblown. For instance, the rise of online retail behemoths like Amazon did disrupt the traditional retail landscape. Some physical stores closed, unable to compete. However, many others adapted and evolved, leveraging the internet to expand their reach, integrate online and offline shopping experiences, and even create new job opportunities.

Similarly, concerns about job displacement were partially valid. Roles involving routine, repetitive tasks were automated or became redundant. But concurrently, the internet birthed a host of new job categories in fields like web design, digital marketing, and cybersecurity.

Privacy, a significant concern during the internet boom, remains a pertinent issue even today. With incidents of data breaches and misuse of personal data, these fears are continually validated. However, these challenges have prompted stronger cybersecurity measures and more stringent data privacy regulations.

The fears that surfaced during the Dotcom Boom bear striking resemblances to those we associate with AI today. Like the internet, AI promises to revolutionize many aspects of our lives, causing uncertainties and sparking fears. Some of these concerns may be realized, but as history has shown us, we also need to remain open to the new opportunities that AI might unveil.

Navigating the future with AI will require acknowledging these fears, learning from the past, and proactively addressing potential issues. Fear and resistance to change are natural responses, but they can be managed effectively through understanding, responsible regulation, and ethical considerations. As we step into an AI-integrated future, remembering these lessons from the past will be key to embracing the promise of AI, while also mitigating its challenges.

Exaggerated Claims and Hype: The Distortion of AI Reality

One of the most significant contributors to the misunderstanding and fear surrounding AI is the cloud of hype that often accompanies its discussion. Companies, in an attempt to seize the spotlight or attract investment, frequently make inflated claims about their AI technologies. This hype can foster unrealistic expectations, leading to misconceptions about what AI can realistically achieve.

The term "AI" itself is a buzzword that has caught the attention of the media, investors, and the public alike. Companies, eager to tap into this excitement, may brand their products as "AI-powered" even when the underlying technology might be a simple algorithm that has been in use for years. The resulting hype can mislead the public into believing that such products possess advanced intelligence, which is often not the case.

Startups in the AI field, in particular, are sometimes guilty of over-promising on their AI capabilities to secure funding. They might present a vision of their technology that far outstrips its current capacities, fostering a belief in an imminent AI revolution. While such promises may help in short-term gain, they contribute to a distorted understanding of AI's actual potential and timeline for advancement.

The media also plays a role in amplifying the hype. Exciting breakthroughs in AI research often get widely reported, with emphasis on their most sensational aspects. However, the nuances, limitations, and caveats of these advancements are typically less prominent, creating an image of AI that is more science fiction than science fact.

The consequence of this exaggeration and hype is a public perception of AI that veers between unrealistic optimism and unfounded dread. On the one hand, people may believe that AI is on the brink of achieving human-like consciousness or that it can solve complex world problems single-handedly. On the other hand, the portrayal of AI as a near-magical technology also fuels fears of its potential to become a malevolent force or render humans obsolete.

Recognizing and addressing this hype is essential in promoting a balanced and accurate understanding of AI. It's important for companies, researchers, and the media to present a realistic picture of AI's capabilities and limitations, and for the public to critically assess the information they receive. As we progress further into the era of AI, distinguishing the fact from the fiction will be increasingly critical.

By understanding why these misconceptions and fears exist, we can work towards dispelling them and fostering a more accurate and nuanced understanding of AI. As with any technology, a clear and realistic understanding of AI is essential for its responsible and effective use. This includes acknowledging both its potential benefits and its limitations, as well as the ethical and societal implications of its use.

Chapter 3: AI in Action Today - A Cross-Industry Overview

Artificial Intelligence (AI) is not just a futuristic concept; it's a reality that's transforming industries and economies around the world today. From healthcare to finance, transportation to entertainment, AI's applications are as diverse as they are revolutionary. Let's delve into how AI is being used in various sectors today.

Healthcare

Healthcare is one of the sectors most profoundly influenced by AI. This technology has become an invaluable tool in diagnosing illnesses, predicting disease outbreaks, personalizing treatment plans, and even assisting in surgeries.

Example 1: Diagnosis and Risk Prediction

Machine learning algorithms can analyze vast amounts of data to recognize patterns that might be invisible to the human eye. For instance, AI is being used to read and interpret medical images, such as X-rays, CT scans, and MRIs, to detect conditions like cancer, often with accuracy comparable to or exceeding that of human professionals. These systems can help overburdened healthcare systems by triaging cases, allowing doctors to focus on the most severe cases.

Furthermore, AI can analyze Electronic Health Records (EHRs) and other healthcare data to predict which patients are at risk of developing certain conditions. For instance, Google's DeepMind Health developed an AI system capable of predicting Acute Kidney Injury (AKI) up to 48 hours before it occurs, potentially saving lives and healthcare resources.

Example 2: Precision Medicine

AI is also revolutionizing treatment by enabling more personalized and effective care. Precision medicine involves tailoring treatment based on a patient's unique genetic makeup, lifestyle, and environment. By analyzing vast amounts of genomic data and correlating it with patient outcomes, AI can help identify which treatments are most likely to be effective for individual patients. This approach has been particularly promising in oncology.

Example 3: Robotic Surgery

Robotic surgery is another exciting application of AI. Surgical robots like Intuitive Surgical's da Vinci System allow surgeons to perform complex procedures with increased precision, flexibility, and control. AI enhances these systems by providing real-time imaging analysis during surgery, helping the surgeon navigate and make decisions.

Example 4: Virtual Health Assistants

AI-powered virtual health assistants, such as chatbots, are being used to provide medical advice and monitor patients' health. These systems can analyze symptoms, recommend treatments, remind patients to take their medication, and even alert healthcare providers if a patient's condition worsens. By providing round-the-clock monitoring and support, these systems can improve healthcare outcomes and reduce strain on healthcare providers.

Despite these promising applications, it's important to remember that AI is a tool to assist healthcare professionals, not replace them. AI can analyze data and recognize patterns, but it lacks the human touch, holistic understanding, and empathetic care that healthcare providers offer. The key to AI's successful integration into healthcare lies in the synergy between human expertise and AI's analytical capabilities.

Finance

The financial sector has been quick to harness the power of AI, recognizing its potential to increase efficiency, reduce risk, and enhance customer service. Here's a closer look at how AI is being utilized in finance.

Example 1: Fraud Detection and Prevention

One of the earliest applications of AI in finance was in fraud detection. AI algorithms can analyze millions of transactions in real-time, identifying patterns and anomalies that indicate fraudulent activity. For example, if an account that is typically used for small, local purchases suddenly makes several large purchases overseas, AI can flag the activity for review. This kind of real-time detection was almost impossible with manual methods and has made banking safer for customers and institutions alike.

Example 2: Algorithmic Trading

Algorithmic trading involves using AI systems to buy and sell stocks at optimal prices and times, typically in high-frequency trading environments. These AI algorithms use a variety of data—ranging from market trends and economic news to social media sentiment—to make predictions and execute trades.

Example 3: Robo-Advisors

Robo-advisors are AI applications that provide personalized investment advice to clients. They use machine learning algorithms to analyze a client's financial situation and investment goals and then recommend an optimal portfolio. This makes financial planning and investing more accessible and affordable, as robo-advisors typically charge lower fees than human advisors.

Example 4: Credit Scoring

AI is increasingly being used to make credit scoring more accurate and fair. Traditional credit scoring methods often rely on a limited set of factors and can disadvantage certain groups. AI can analyze a broader range of data—including non-traditional data like mobile phone usage or social media activity—to assess creditworthiness. This can help extend credit to people who might otherwise be excluded by traditional systems.

Despite the promising applications of AI in finance, it's essential to navigate this field with caution. Issues like data privacy, algorithmic bias, and the potential for system errors or misuse need to be carefully considered. AI systems should be used as tools to enhance, not replace, human judgement and oversight.

Transportation

From autonomous vehicles to traffic management systems, AI has been pivotal in the transformation of the transportation sector. The following subsections provide more detail on how AI is reshaping this industry.

Example 1: Autonomous Vehicles

Perhaps the most recognizable application of AI in transportation is in the development of autonomous, or self-driving, vehicles. Companies like Tesla, Waymo, and Uber are investing heavily in this technology. These vehicles use an array of sensors, cameras, and AI algorithms to perceive their surroundings, interpret traffic rules, make decisions, and navigate their environment safely. While fully autonomous vehicles are still not widespread as of now, the progress in this area is substantial.

Example 2: Traffic Management

AI is also being used to optimize traffic management systems in cities around the world. By analyzing data from traffic cameras, sensors, GPS devices, and social media, AI systems can predict traffic conditions and manage traffic lights to reduce congestion and improve flow. This can reduce travel times, save fuel, and decrease emissions.

Example 3: Public Transportation

In the realm of public transportation, AI is used to optimize routes and schedules, making public transit more efficient and reliable. Predictive maintenance, enabled by AI, can anticipate issues with vehicles or infrastructure before they cause delays. AI-powered chatbots are also being used to provide real-time updates to passengers, improving the user experience.

Example 4: Logistics and Supply Chain

AI has significant implications for logistics and supply chain operations within the transportation industry. For instance, AI can optimize delivery routes, considering factors like traffic, weather, and package destination. Predictive analytics can forecast demand, helping businesses manage inventory efficiently. Autonomous vehicles, including drones and trucks, are being used to automate deliveries, especially for the "last mile."

Example 5: Maritime and Aviation

In maritime and aviation, AI is being used for route optimization, fuel efficiency, and predictive maintenance. Autonomous technology is also on the rise, with AI-powered drones and autonomous ships becoming more prevalent.

While AI holds immense potential for improving efficiency, safety, and sustainability in transportation, it also brings challenges. These include technological hurdles, regulatory questions, and issues related to job displacement and security. As with other sectors, it's essential to approach these challenges with a thoughtful and balanced perspective.

Entertainment

AI has become a critical tool in the creation, distribution, and consumption of entertainment content. It's reshaping the landscape of music, film, gaming, and other forms of media, enabling new experiences and efficiencies.

Example 1: Content Creation

AI is being used to assist in creating entertainment content. In the film industry, for example, AI can automate certain aspects of editing, create realistic CGI, and even generate story ideas. It's also being used in the music industry, where AI algorithms can compose music or assist musicians in developing new melodies or harmonies.

Example 2: Recommendation Systems

Recommendation systems are one of the most visible applications of AI in entertainment. Companies like Netflix, Amazon, and Spotify use AI to analyze user behavior and suggest content tailored to individual tastes. These systems consider a wide range of factors, from viewing history to time spent on specific content, to deliver increasingly personalized recommendations.

Example 3: Virtual Reality (VR) and Augmented Reality (AR)

AI plays a crucial role in VR and AR, technologies that are increasingly popular in gaming and interactive experiences. AI can generate realistic, responsive characters and environments, enhancing the immersion and realism of these experiences.

Example 4: Targeted Advertising

AI's data analysis capabilities are used in targeted advertising, a significant revenue source in the entertainment industry. By analyzing user data, AI can deliver personalized ads that are more likely to resonate with the viewer, thereby increasing engagement and effectiveness.

Example 5: Deepfakes and Synthetic Media

AI can generate deepfakes and synthetic media—highly realistic, AI-generated audiovisual content that can mimic real people. This has potential applications in film and TV production but also raises significant ethical and legal concerns about consent, misinformation, and digital identity.

Despite the exciting possibilities, AI's role in entertainment also brings challenges, including job displacement fears, data privacy concerns, and the potential misuse of technologies like deepfakes. Ensuring an ethical and responsible approach to AI in entertainment is paramount as we navigate this new era.

Retail

AI is reshaping the retail landscape, offering opportunities to enhance customer experiences, optimize operations, and increase sales. Here are some of the ways AI is being used in retail.

Example 1: Personalization

AI is playing a key role in personalizing the shopping experience. Retailers use AI algorithms to analyze customer data and shopping behavior, providing tailored product recommendations, personalized promotions, and targeted marketing campaigns. This can significantly enhance customer satisfaction and increase sales.

Example 2: Inventory Management

AI is used in inventory management to predict demand, optimize stock levels, and reduce waste. Machine learning algorithms can analyze historical sales data, current market trends, and even external factors like weather or holidays to forecast product demand. This helps retailers ensure they have the right products available at the right time, minimizing both stockouts and overstocks.

Example 3: Chatbots and Virtual Assistants

AI-powered chatbots and virtual assistants are being used to provide customer service in online retail environments. These systems can answer common customer inquiries, assist with purchases, and provide after-sales support. This not only enhances the customer experience but also reduces the burden on human customer service representatives.

Example 4: Price Optimization

AI can help retailers optimize their pricing strategies. By analyzing data on sales history, competitor pricing, customer demand, and market trends, AI can recommend pricing strategies that maximize revenue and profit.

Example 5: Store Layout and Design

In physical retail spaces, AI can analyze customer behavior to optimize store layout and product placement. This can involve tracking customer movements within a store, analyzing which products are viewed or purchased together, and adjusting layouts to improve sales and customer satisfaction.

Example 6: Fraud Detection

AI is used in the retail industry to detect and prevent fraudulent transactions. AI systems can analyze patterns in transaction data to identify suspicious activity and flag it for further investigation.

While AI offers considerable benefits for the retail industry, it also presents challenges, including data privacy and security concerns, the potential for job displacement, and issues related to bias in AI algorithms. As with other industries, it's critical to approach these challenges with careful consideration and ethical guidelines.

Education

Education is undergoing a digital transformation, and AI is at the forefront of this change. From personalized learning to administrative efficiency, AI is enabling more effective, engaging, and inclusive educational experiences. Here's a closer look at how AI is being used in education.

Example 1: Intelligent Tutoring Systems

One of the most significant applications of AI in education is in Intelligent Tutoring Systems (ITS). These systems use AI algorithms to provide personalized instruction based on a student's unique needs. They can adapt the pace of instruction, provide targeted feedback, and suggest resources that align with the student's learning style and proficiency level. This personalized approach can lead to improved learning outcomes.

Example 2: Automated Grading

AI can automate the grading of tests and assignments, saving educators significant time and ensuring more consistent evaluations. While currently most effective with multiple-choice or fill-in-the-blank tests, advances in Natural Language Processing (NLP) are enhancing AI's ability to grade more complex, written responses.

Example 3: Predictive Analytics

AI can analyze data on students' academic performance and learning behaviors to predict future outcomes. These insights can help identify at-risk students early on, allowing for timely intervention. It can also help in course planning, optimizing class sizes, and resource allocation.

Example 4: AI-driven Content Development

AI is being used to develop educational content that adapts to a learner's needs. For instance, AI can generate quizzes based on a student's performance or suggest further reading materials when a student struggles with a specific concept. AI can also create engaging learning experiences with virtual reality (VR) and augmented reality (AR) simulations.

Example 5: Administrative Tasks Automation

AI can automate administrative tasks, such as scheduling, admissions, and record-keeping, reducing the administrative burden on educators and allowing them to focus more on their students.

Despite these promising applications, the use of AI in education also raises questions about data privacy, the digital divide, and the role of human teachers. It's important to ensure that AI is used ethically and equitably, and that it enhances, rather than replaces, the human touch in education.

All the examples represent just a fraction of AI's current applications across industries. In each case, AI not only improves efficiency and outcomes but also opens up new possibilities and models of operation.

The following sections will dive deeper into these industries, exploring the transformative impact of AI and the potential it holds for the future.

AI's Achievements and Limitations

AI's recent achievements have been impressive and transformative. Yet, while AI's potential is enormous, it's equally important to recognize its current limitations. This section explores the key accomplishments and inherent constraints of AI.

AI's accomplishments span various sectors, bringing about improvements in efficiency, productivity, and often even new capabilities that were previously thought impossible.

AI's *Achievements*:

1. Natural Language Processing (NLP): AI's ability to understand, generate, and respond to human language has improved tremendously. NLP allows AI to perform tasks like translation, sentiment analysis, and even writing articles or reports.

2. Image and Voice Recognition: AI's proficiency in recognizing images and voices has led to breakthroughs in areas like healthcare (for disease diagnosis), autonomous vehicles (for object detection and avoidance), and smart home devices (voice-controlled systems like Amazon's Alexa or Google Home).

3. Predictive Analysis: AI's predictive capabilities have revolutionized sectors like finance (for forecasting stock trends), marketing (for predicting consumer behavior), and even climate science (for predicting weather patterns and climate change effects).

4. Game Playing: AI has achieved remarkable feats in complex games. Google's AlphaGo defeated a world champion Go player, a game considered much more complex than chess. OpenAI's Chat GPT-3 and GPT-4 showcase an impressive ability to generate human-like text, fooling many into thinking they were interacting with a human or something of human like intelligence.

Despite these accomplishments, AI also has important *Limitations* to consider:

1. Lack of Common-Sense Understanding: AI systems, even those that perform impressively on specific tasks, lack a general understanding of the world. They can't make sense of things the way humans do, and they can make errors that appear bizarre to a human observer.

2. Dependency on Data: AI systems, particularly machine learning models, require vast amounts of data to learn. They are only as good as the data they are trained on, and biased or incomplete data can lead to biased or inaccurate outcomes.

3. Transparency and Explainability: Often, AI systems operate as "black boxes," making decisions without clearly explaining how they arrived at them. This lack of transparency can be problematic in fields where accountability is crucial.

4. Lack of Emotional Intelligence: Despite advances in NLP and voice recognition, AI systems lack true emotional intelligence. They can't understand or respond to human emotions in the nuanced way that humans can.

5. Job Displacement Concerns: AI automation raises concerns about job displacement. While AI can create new jobs, it can also render certain roles obsolete, raising important societal and ethical issues.

Understanding both the achievements and limitations of AI is crucial for harnessing its potential responsibly and effectively.

Classifications of AI

Artificial intelligence can be broadly classified into two types: Narrow AI and General AI, also known as Artificial General Intelligence (AGI). A third concept, Superintelligent AI, describes a hypothetical future state of AGI.

Narrow AI: *Power in Specificity*

The artificial intelligence systems that are part and parcel of our everyday lives - from song recommendations on Spotify and facial recognition on Facebook to navigation instructions from Google Maps and automated driving in Tesla cars - belong to a category known as Narrow AI, or Weak AI.

Narrow AI is specifically designed to perform a particular task or a set of tasks. It excels in its specific domain, like playing the game of chess, identifying spam emails, translating languages, or diagnosing medical conditions based on MRI scans. However, its scope of operation is strictly limited to the tasks it has been trained to do. It doesn't possess understanding, consciousness, or the ability to apply learned knowledge to tasks outside its purview.

Despite being labelled 'narrow' or 'weak', these AI systems can be incredibly sophisticated and capable within their specific domains. Google's AlphaGo, a Narrow AI designed for playing the board game Go, stunned the world in 2016 by defeating a world champion Go player. AlphaGo's success stemmed from its proficiency in a single, narrowly defined task: playing Go.

Narrow AI operates based on predefined rules, algorithms, and statistical patterns. For instance, a song-recommending AI might analyze a user's listening history, compare it with the listening habits of millions of other users, and use this data to suggest songs the user might like. The AI doesn't 'understand' music or the user's taste in the way a human would; it simply identifies patterns and applies them to make predictions.

The crucial point to grasp about Narrow AI is that it doesn't possess general intelligence. It doesn't have the capability to understand, learn, adapt, and apply its knowledge across a wide range of tasks like a human. It's 'intelligent' only within its specific task domain.

Recognizing the limitations of Narrow AI helps to dispel fears and misconceptions about AI taking over the world or making humans obsolete. It's also key to understanding where we are currently in terms of AI development and what the path to more advanced forms of AI might look like. While Narrow AI is already transforming numerous industries and aspects of our daily lives, it's just one piece of the larger AI puzzle.

General AI: *The Horizon of Potential*

While Narrow AI is specialized to excel in specific tasks, another concept in AI, known as General AI or Artificial General Intelligence (AGI), represents a different level of AI capability altogether. Unlike Narrow AI, AGI refers to a type of AI that possesses the ability to understand, learn, adapt, and implement knowledge across a wide range of tasks that a human being can do. It encapsulates the idea of a system that can apply intelligence in a flexible and generalized manner, similar to human intelligence.

In essence, an AGI system wouldn't just be an expert in one specific domain but would have the capability to transfer knowledge from one domain to another, learn new tasks with minimal human intervention, understand context, and make decisions based on ambiguous and incomplete information - a much more advanced version of AI than what we currently have.

For instance, while a Narrow AI might be a grandmaster at chess, an AGI would have the capability to be a grandmaster at chess, understand and converse in any human language, write a compelling novel, invent a scientific theory, cook a delicious meal, and even understand emotions and social cues - all while being able to learn new skills and improve over time.

It's important to note, however, that AGI is currently a theoretical concept. As of the current state of AI development, we have yet to create an AI system that demonstrates the breadth of capabilities implied by AGI. Achieving AGI is considered a holy grail of sorts in AI research.

The prospect of AGI presents a fascinating, yet challenging, milestone. The development of AGI could potentially lead to systems that perform tasks more efficiently than humans, given their ability to process vast amounts of information quickly, accurately, and without fatigue. However, the attainment of AGI also raises complex ethical and societal issues that need careful consideration and robust frameworks to handle.

Understanding the distinction between Narrow AI and General AI is essential. It provides context to current AI capabilities, sets expectations for future developments, and helps to address some of the fears and misconceptions about AI's potential and risks. While Narrow AI is already creating significant changes in our lives and societies, the advent of AGI would represent a paradigm shift in human history.

Superintelligent AI: *Beyond Human Limitations*

After Narrow AI and General AI, the next tier on the scale of theoretical artificial intelligence is Superintelligent AI. This concept, initially introduced by philosopher Nick Bostrom, refers to an AI that doesn't just mirror human intellectual capabilities but significantly surpasses them. This form of AI would vastly exceed human performance across an extensive range of tasks and fields.

Imagine a chess grandmaster AI, but instead of being solely specialized in chess, it could outperform the best human experts in virtually every economically or academically relevant field - from scientific research and medical diagnosis to artistic creativity and business strategy. Such an AI wouldn't just replicate human intelligence; it would redefine the boundaries of knowledge and capabilities.

In a world of Superintelligent AI, the pace of scientific and technological innovation could accelerate exponentially, with AI making discoveries and solving problems that are currently beyond human comprehension. The rate of change would be so rapid that it could result in a dramatic shift in human society and civilization.

However, along with this grand vision of accelerated innovation and problem-solving, Superintelligent AI also presents significant potential risks and ethical concerns. The core of these concerns lies in control and alignment. Can we maintain control of a system that is, by definition, vastly more intelligent than we are? Can we ensure that it aligns with our values and goals, especially when it could potentially redefine those goals with its superior understanding?

The concept of Superintelligent AI also raises fundamental questions about our place in the world. If machines surpass us in intellectual capabilities, what does it mean for us as a species? These complex issues and more will be explored in the subsequent chapters of this book.

While Superintelligent AI remains a hypothetical concept as of now, understanding its possibilities, as well as its implications, is crucial. It prepares us to navigate potential future scenarios and stimulates important discussions that need to be had to ensure responsible and beneficial advancement of AI technology. The journey to Superintelligent AI, if we ever embark on it, will be filled with unprecedented opportunities and challenges. Therefore, our approach towards it should be one of cautious optimism, underscored by proactive preparedness and thoughtful dialogue.

Understanding these distinctions between Narrow AI, General AI, and Superintelligent AI is crucial in any discussion about the potential, realities, and future of AI. It provides context to both the accomplishments we've seen and the challenges and concerns that lie ahead.

Chapter 4 The Future of AI: Predictions and Possibilities

As we peer into the horizon, the evolution of AI unfurls a mesmerizing tapestry of forecasts and potentialities. The escalating sophistication of AI technologies, bolstered by swift strides in computing power and the burgeoning abundance of data, hints at a future where transformative changes sweep across a multitude of sectors.

With each technological breakthrough, AI is set to become an even more ingrained aspect of our daily lives, steering us towards an era characterized by Ubiquitous AI. This extensive integration is expected to manifest across various strata, from the intricacies of personal devices and home automation to the grander scale of societal infrastructures, including transportation and healthcare systems.

As we navigate this exciting trajectory, it's critical to acknowledge and prepare for the transformative potential that AI holds for our future. The possibilities are expansive and only limited by our collective imagination, aspiration, and our willingness to steer the course of AI in a way that augments and enriches the human experience.

AI in Our Homes: The Dawn of the Smart Home Era

In recent years, we've begun to experience the first wave of AI making its way into our homes. Devices like the Amazon Echo or Google Home, powered by AI voice assistants, have rapidly evolved from novelty items to commonplace household fixtures. They can play our favorite music, update us on the weather, control our lights, and even tell us jokes, all on command. But this is just the beginning.

As AI continues to advance, the concept of a 'smart home' will take on new dimensions. It won't just be about isolated devices responding to our immediate commands. Instead, AI will interweave with our daily routines, transforming our homes into integrated, anticipatory environments.

Appliances and devices will communicate with each other and with us, learning our patterns, preferences, and needs. Your refrigerator, for instance, could monitor its contents and alert you when you're running low on certain items. It could even suggest recipes based on the ingredients available, helping to minimize food waste. Similarly, your thermostat could learn your schedule and adjust room temperatures according to your daily routines, ensuring a comfortable home environment while optimizing energy use.

Furthermore, smart home technology could also enhance home security, with AI-powered cameras and alarm systems that can distinguish between normal and suspicious activity. These systems could provide real-time alerts and updates, offering peace of mind, especially when you're away from home.

The implications of AI in our homes extend beyond convenience and security. For instance, smart home technology could play a pivotal role in healthcare, particularly for the elderly or those with chronic illnesses. With AI-powered health monitoring systems, people could receive timely care and intervention, reducing the need for hospital visits and improving quality of life.

While the idea of AI-powered homes might raise privacy concerns, with appropriate regulation and transparency, the benefits could significantly outweigh potential risks. As we continue to usher in this era of smart homes, we're not just upgrading our living spaces; we're redefining our everyday lives. The home of the future, powered by AI, promises to be a place that's more connected, convenient, and attuned to our needs than ever before.

AI in Our Work: Revolutionizing the Workplace

The integration of AI in our work environments is no longer a distant projection; it's a transformation that's already underway. As this evolution accelerates, it is set to redefine how we work, collaborate, and strive towards productivity and innovation.

At the forefront of this revolution are AI-powered virtual assistants. As these systems evolve, they will assume more advanced roles than merely scheduling appointments or setting reminders. They will sift through our inboxes, prioritizing crucial emails and filtering out spam. They will also assist with complex tasks such as data analysis, report generation, and even drafting responses or documents, freeing up time for us to focus on creative, strategic, and interpersonal aspects of our jobs.

Simultaneously, AI is also expected to revolutionize remote work and virtual collaboration, a development made increasingly relevant in the wake of a global shift towards remote and hybrid work models. Virtual meeting platforms could leverage AI to enhance audio and video quality, provide real-time transcription and translation services, and even analyze meeting data to suggest improvements in efficiency and engagement. AI could also help manage distributed teams, tracking project progress, and predicting potential roadblocks or delays.

Beyond these applications, AI holds the potential to reshape industry-specific workflows and tasks. In healthcare, AI could assist in diagnosing diseases, predicting patient outcomes, and personalizing treatment plans. In education, AI-powered systems could offer customized learning pathways for students, dynamically adapting to their strengths and areas for improvement. For the finance sector, AI could enhance fraud detection, automate trading strategies, and provide personalized investment advice.

Yet, while the infiltration of AI in our workplaces promises numerous benefits, it also presents challenges. Job displacement due to automation, concerns about surveillance, and the necessity for continuous upskilling are issues that will need to be addressed. Additionally, the potential for AI systems to reflect and perpetuate existing biases, particularly in decision-making roles, must be considered and mitigated.

Therefore, as we navigate this shift, it will be crucial to foster a balanced, inclusive dialogue about the ethical implications and societal impact of AI in our work. Through thoughtful and proactive planning, we can shape a future where AI doesn't replace humans, but complements and elevates human potential, paving the way for a more productive and innovative work environment.

AI in Public Spaces: *Building the Cities of the Future*

As AI continues to evolve and become more sophisticated, it will progressively pervade our public spaces, offering the potential to enhance efficiency, safety, and sustainability. The concept of 'smart cities,' urban areas that use different types of electronic methods and sensors to collect data, is becoming a reality with AI as the linchpin.

AI's applications in urban settings are multifaceted. For instance, in the realm of transportation, AI can help manage and coordinate traffic flow more efficiently. Intelligent traffic management systems, fueled by AI algorithms, could analyze real-time traffic data, predict congestion, and dynamically adjust traffic signals to optimize vehicle flow. Additionally, autonomous vehicles guided by AI could reshape public transportation, reducing human error, and increasing efficiency.

In the domain of energy, AI could facilitate smarter energy usage, helping cities become more sustainable. AI systems could predict and adjust to energy demands, control smart grids to minimize energy wastage, and optimize renewable energy sources. Through these applications, AI could play a critical role in reducing our carbon footprint and tackling climate change.

AI's potential in enhancing public safety and security is significant. Advanced surveillance systems equipped with AI can monitor public spaces for unusual activities, improving response times in emergencies. AI could also help in predictive policing, using data to anticipate crime hotspots, although this usage comes with significant ethical considerations around privacy and bias.

Waste management, another critical urban service, could also benefit from AI. Intelligent systems could optimize waste collection routes, reduce operational costs, and even predict waste generation patterns, aiding in planning and resource allocation.

Moreover, AI could transform the maintenance of public infrastructure. Predictive maintenance algorithms can process data from sensors embedded in infrastructure like bridges, roads, and public buildings, forecasting potential structural issues before they become critical, thereby improving safety and reducing repair costs.

While the infiltration of AI in our public spaces promises numerous benefits, it also brings challenges and ethical considerations. Issues around data privacy, surveillance, and the potential for algorithmic bias must be addressed as part of the move towards AI-powered public spaces. Therefore, as we embrace the potential of AI to enhance our cities, we must do so with a commitment to ethical guidelines and regulations that protect citizens' rights and interests. As we move forward into an increasingly AI-driven world, the goal should be not only smarter cities but also more equitable, inclusive, and sustainable ones.

AI in Personal Devices: *Enhancing Daily Life and Personal Health*
Artificial intelligence is becoming an integral component of our personal devices, shaping our daily lives in profound ways. Today, AI is a cornerstone technology in smartphones, smartwatches, fitness trackers, and is gradually making its way into more personal devices, including smart clothing and potentially even implantable tech. As AI becomes even more pervasive, it promises to transform our interactions, improve our health, and even augment our abilities.

Smartphones are a prime example of how AI has already begun to improve our daily lives. AI-powered virtual assistants like Siri, Google Assistant, and Alexa are now commonplace, helping us manage our schedules, answer questions, and perform a myriad of tasks hands-free. AI algorithms also power recommendation systems on our devices, suggesting music, movies, or products based on our preferences and habits.

Looking forward, AI is set to further revolutionize the capabilities of our personal devices. For instance, smartphones and smartwatches could use AI to provide even more personalized services. By learning from our behavior and preferences, these devices could offer insights, recommendations, and alerts tailored to our unique needs and lifestyle.

One exciting area is health monitoring. AI algorithms can analyze data from wearable fitness trackers and smartwatches to monitor our heart rate, sleep patterns, activity levels, and more. By detecting anomalies and patterns in these biometrics, AI can provide insights about our health and even alert us to potential health issues before they become severe. Wearable tech could also aid in managing chronic conditions, reminding patients to take medication or alerting them to potential triggers.

The advent of smart clothing – garments embedded with sensors – promises to take health monitoring a step further. These garments could track a wider range of biometrics in real-time, providing a more comprehensive picture of our health and wellbeing. Powered by AI, these devices could analyze this data to offer personalized health and fitness advice.

Looking further into the future, we might see the rise of implantable technology, bringing AI even closer to us. While this may sound like science fiction, research is already underway. These devices could provide real-time health monitoring, early disease detection, and perhaps even augment our physical or cognitive capabilities. However, such advances also raise significant ethical and privacy concerns that must be carefully addressed.

As AI continues to permeate our personal devices, it is crucial to balance the potential benefits with privacy considerations. The vast amount of personal data these devices collect makes robust data security measures and clear privacy policies more important than ever. Therefore, as we embrace the conveniences and benefits of AI in our personal devices, we must also advocate for responsible practices that protect our data and our privacy.

Challenges and Considerations: Navigating the Complexities of the AI Landscape

As AI becomes increasingly prevalent in our lives, it brings not only benefits but also significant challenges. These issues span from data privacy and security to algorithmic bias, and the widening digital divide. If left unaddressed, these challenges can impede the positive potential of AI and even perpetuate harm. As we navigate the new AI-infused landscape, it is imperative to tackle these issues head-on, ensuring a fair, ethical, and sustainable deployment of AI technologies.

Data privacy and security is one of the most pressing challenges in the AI era. AI systems often rely on large volumes of data for their operation, and much of this data is personal. The collection, storage, and analysis of this data raise critical questions about privacy. Who has access to the data? How is it used and stored? What safeguards are in place to prevent misuse or breaches? As we embed AI more deeply in our lives, it's crucial to have robust data protection frameworks in place, along with clear and transparent data policies.

Algorithmic bias presents another significant challenge. AI systems learn from the data they are trained on, which means they can inadvertently perpetuate biases present in that data. For instance, an AI system trained on biased hiring data might propagate those biases by favoring certain demographics over others. Algorithmic bias can have serious real-world consequences, leading to unfair outcomes in critical areas such as hiring, lending, law enforcement, and healthcare. Addressing algorithmic bias requires rigorous testing, transparent reporting, and ongoing monitoring of AI systems.

The digital divide, the gap between those who have access to technology and those who don't, is another critical issue in the age of AI. As AI technologies become more embedded in our daily lives, those who lack access risk being left behind, exacerbating social and economic inequalities. Bridging the digital divide requires concerted effort and investment in infrastructure, affordable access, digital literacy, and inclusive design.

The rise of AI also brings forth ethical considerations. AI systems are increasingly making decisions or recommendations that affect people's lives, yet the decision-making processes of these systems are often opaque, a situation referred to as the "black box" problem of AI. As we entrust AI with more responsibilities, we need to ensure the accountability, transparency, and fairness of these systems.

These challenges underscore the need for thoughtful governance and regulation of AI technologies. As we integrate AI more into our lives, we need to ensure that this is done in a manner that respects privacy, promotes fairness, bridges the digital divide, and upholds ethical standards. Policymakers, technologists, and society at large all have a role to play in shaping the AI landscape to ensure it serves the common good.

The era of Ubiquitous AI promises a future where AI is not just a tool we use, but a constant companion that shapes our daily experiences and interactions. As we continue to explore this future, we must also consider how we can guide the development of AI in a way that aligns with our values, needs, and aspirations.

Advances in Narrow AI

While discussions about the future of AI often gravitate towards the speculative realm of AGI, it's important to remember that Narrow AI – the type of AI that we interact with in our daily lives – will continue to advance significantly. These advances, occurring in several areas, are set to bring about substantial improvements in efficiency, accuracy, and capabilities.

Deep Learning and Neural Networks: *The Engine Powering Modern AI*
The core of many breakthroughs in contemporary Narrow AI is the concept of deep learning, a subclass of machine learning that draws

inspiration from the human brain's neural networks. As we propel research in this exciting domain, we can anticipate the advent of increasingly sophisticated models. These models, characterized by their capacity to learn from enormous quantities of data, will offer increasingly precise outcomes, impacting a broad array of fields.

Deep learning employs structures known as artificial neural networks (ANNs), which mimic the biological neural networks in our brains. An artificial neural network consists of layers of interconnected nodes or "neurons." Each node takes in input, applies a function to it, and passes the output to the next layer. A neural network "learns" by adjusting the weights and biases within these functions based on the error of its predictions. The depth of these layers in a network is where deep learning gets its name.

A specific type of artificial neural network that has demonstrated extraordinary success is the Convolutional Neural Network (CNN). These networks are uniquely effective at processing visual data, making them pivotal in tasks such as image and video recognition. CNNs feature layers that automatically and adaptively learn spatial hierarchies of features. They work by "scanning" an image with a filter that identifies important features such as edges or specific textures. This technique reduces the complexity of the image while maintaining the features essential for recognition.

Another key artificial neural network architecture in the realm of deep learning is the Recurrent Neural Network (RNN). Unlike traditional neural networks, RNNs have 'memory' in the form of loops that allow information to be passed from one step in the network to the next. This characteristic makes RNNs especially suitable for tasks involving sequential data, such as speech recognition or language translation.

These AI technologies, from deep learning to specialized neural networks like CNNs and RNNs, are set to enhance and evolve continuously. As they become even more efficient and accurate, we can expect them to catalyze further advancements in AI, pushing the boundaries of what's possible. Whether it's improving healthcare diagnostics, making self-driving cars safer, or enhancing our virtual assistants, these technologies will continue to reshape our world.

Reinforcement Learning: *From Games to Real-World Applications*
Reinforcement Learning (RL) is another fascinating area in the machine learning landscape that holds remarkable promise for the future. Distinguished from other types of machine learning, reinforcement

learning focuses on decision-making. An artificial agent learns how to navigate an environment to achieve a specific goal. The agent doesn't just passively receive input and output; instead, it continuously interacts with its environment, learning from its actions based on feedback.

Reinforcement learning is modeled as a Markov Decision Process. It works on the principle of reward and penalty. For every action the agent takes, it receives feedback in the form of a reward (positive reinforcement) or penalty (negative reinforcement). Over time, the agent learns to make decisions that maximize its cumulative reward. This learning methodology enables the agent to understand the long-term consequences of its actions and adapt its behavior to achieve its goal more efficiently.

A classic example of reinforcement learning is its application in games, such as Chess or Go. Google's DeepMind utilized reinforcement learning to train its AlphaGo program, which made headlines in 2016 by defeating a world champion Go player. By playing millions of games against itself, AlphaGo learned to recognize valuable strategies and maneuvers, resulting in an AI player with superhuman Go-playing abilities.

The potential applications of reinforcement learning extend beyond gaming. It can be used in any situation where decision-making over time is crucial. In the realm of autonomous vehicles, for instance, reinforcement learning can be used to train systems to make safe and efficient driving decisions based on real-time traffic conditions.

Moreover, reinforcement learning could revolutionize resource allocation tasks. For instance, in telecommunication networks, reinforcement learning algorithms can be employed to efficiently manage and allocate bandwidth among users, thereby enhancing network performance.

In business scenarios, reinforcement learning can play a significant role in areas like price optimization, inventory management, and even negotiation. A trained AI could learn to negotiate deals or contracts, understanding the trade-offs and long-term benefits of different negotiation strategies.

Advancements in reinforcement learning will likely herald a new generation of Narrow AI systems, systems capable of mastering intricate tasks and making informed, long-term decisions autonomously. As research in this field continues, we may soon witness its influence in various aspects of our lives, from the technology we use daily to the way businesses and economies function.

***Transfer Learning**: Paving the Path to Efficiency*

In the universe of machine learning, a concept has been steadily gaining traction for its potential to revolutionize the way AI systems learn: Transfer Learning. As the name suggests, transfer learning is a method where knowledge acquired from one problem is used to solve a different but related problem. It's akin to a human leveraging knowledge learned in one context to a different but related situation – for example, applying the critical thinking skills learned in chess to strategic business decision-making.

The potential benefits of transfer learning are manifold. Firstly, it paves the path to more efficient AI systems. Traditional machine learning models typically start learning from scratch, requiring significant amounts of data and computational resources to achieve satisfactory performance. In contrast, transfer learning allows an AI system to kickstart its learning process with pre-existing knowledge, thereby requiring less data and computational power.

This aspect of transfer learning is particularly useful in scenarios where data is scarce or expensive to obtain. For example, in medical imaging analysis, getting a large amount of labeled data can be challenging due to privacy issues and the cost involved in expert labeling. Transfer learning can be a game-changer in such situations, enabling the development of powerful AI models with relatively less data.

Secondly, transfer learning could be a stepping stone towards more adaptable AI systems. In the real world, situations change, and new problems often have some degree of similarity to past problems. An AI system that can transfer knowledge from one task to another can adapt to new tasks more quickly and effectively.

One prominent application of transfer learning can be seen in Natural Language Processing (NLP). Models like BERT or GPT-2 are pre-trained on large text corpora to understand the intricacies of language and can then be fine-tuned on specific tasks like sentiment analysis or text summarization with much less data than would otherwise be required.

Looking forward, transfer learning is likely to become even more significant as we strive to build AI systems that can learn more efficiently and adapt to a wide range of tasks. Just as humans draw on past experiences to tackle new problems, AI systems will be expected to use their learned knowledge to efficiently navigate new challenges.

***Interpretability and Transparency**: Opening the "Black Box"*

As Artificial Intelligence continues to permeate our lives, one aspect of its progression is coming under greater scrutiny: the interpretability and transparency of AI systems. Today, many of the cutting-edge AI models, such as deep neural networks, are often referred to as "black boxes." This is because while these models are incredibly good at what they do – be it recognizing faces, understanding speech, or diagnosing diseases – the decision-making processes that they employ are not easily understood by humans.

As the power of AI grows, so does the impact of its decisions. AI systems are now involved in high-stakes domains such as healthcare, where they assist in diagnosing diseases; finance, where they play roles in credit scoring and algorithmic trading; and even the judicial system, where they help in risk assessments of convicts. In these critical situations, it's not enough for an AI system to make a decision – we need to understand why it made that decision.

However, the path towards interpretability and transparency in AI isn't straightforward. The complexity that makes these AI systems so potent also makes them hard to understand. Unraveling this complexity to make AI decision-making more transparent is a significant challenge and one of the most important areas of research in AI today.

The benefits of a more interpretable and transparent AI are manifold. For one, it enhances trust in AI systems. If users, be they doctors, loan officers, or ordinary individuals, understand why an AI is making a particular decision, they're more likely to trust it. Additionally, it promotes fairness and accountability. If an AI system makes a mistake or shows bias, understanding the system's decision-making process can help pinpoint the issue and correct it.

In terms of practical applications, methods like Local Interpretable Model-Agnostic Explanations (LIME) or Shapley Additive Explanations (SHAP) are already being used to shed light on AI decision-making. These methods attempt to explain the predictions of any machine learning model in a way that humans can understand.

Looking forward, as we strive to build AI systems that are not only more powerful but also beneficial to all of humanity, the pursuit of interpretability and transparency will become increasingly important. By opening the "black box," we can ensure that AI is not only a tool of great power but also of great understanding.

***Interdisciplinary AI**: Building Bridges Across Fields*

As we step further into the age of Narrow AI, the boundaries separating AI from other scientific disciplines are becoming increasingly blurred. This intermingling is both necessary and exciting, as it holds the promise of yielding more sophisticated AI systems, capable of tackling real-world challenges with unprecedented efficiency.

The growing need for an interdisciplinary approach to AI stems from the recognition that intelligence, whether artificial or natural, is not confined to one domain. It is a multifaceted phenomenon, influenced by myriad factors that span across diverse scientific fields. By leveraging insights from these different domains, we can deepen our understanding of intelligence, enrich the theoretical frameworks underlying AI, and develop more nuanced and versatile AI models.

Neuroscience, the study of the brain and nervous system, offers a wellspring of insights that can be harnessed to enhance AI. From the intricate workings of neural circuits to the larger dynamics of brain networks, these biological phenomena have inspired several pivotal AI advancements, including the concept of artificial neural networks and deep learning.

Similarly, insights from cognitive science and psychology, fields that explore the mind and behavior, can enrich AI. These domains provide a profound understanding of perception, learning, memory, and decision-making, all of which can guide the development of AI systems that better emulate these human cognitive processes.

Even the field of social sciences, which may seem removed from the realm of AI, can offer valuable contributions. As AI systems become more embedded in our society, understanding the societal, economic, and cultural contexts in which these systems operate becomes crucial. This can help to ensure that AI not only works efficiently but also aligns with human values and societal norms.

A particularly striking manifestation of this interdisciplinary trend is the field of AI ethics. This burgeoning discipline, situated at the crossroads of AI, philosophy, law, and social sciences, seeks to address the ethical and societal implications of AI, ensuring that its development and deployment are beneficial for all.

In the future of Narrow AI, the fusion of AI with these and other disciplines is set to become more pronounced. As researchers, engineers, and innovators from varied fields collaborate, they'll shape an era of AI that's not only more sophisticated but also more attuned to the multifaceted nature of intelligence and the complexity of the world it seeks to navigate. Interdisciplinary AI represents the exciting journey towards building machines that are not just intelligent but also insightful, adaptable, and beneficial for humanity.

While it's exciting to imagine a future with AGI or Superintelligent AI, it's the advances in Narrow AI that will have the most immediate and tangible impacts on our lives. As these systems become more sophisticated, they will continue to transform industries, change the way we work, and shape our daily experiences.

Progress Towards AGI

Artificial General Intelligence (AGI), a form of AI that can perform any *intellectual* task that a human can, is often seen as the holy grail of AI research. Despite being a distant goal, progress is being made, and the steps toward this milestone could have profound implications.

Foundational Research: *The Building Blocks of AGI*

Achieving Artificial General Intelligence (AGI) is a complex and multifaceted challenge. It requires a deep understanding of both the technical and conceptual aspects of intelligence, and the marrying of these perspectives in a way that allows for the creation of a system that can adapt and reason across a broad range of tasks. Foundational research in various subfields of AI, including but not limited to machine learning, cognitive science, and neuroscience, lays the groundwork for this endeavor.

Machine learning is undoubtedly at the heart of this journey. It's the driving force behind most AI advancements we see today, and its role in the pursuit of AGI is equally crucial. The key is to develop machine learning algorithms and models that are not just proficient in specific tasks, but also capable of generalized learning. This would entail an ability to apply knowledge gleaned from one task to a different, yet related, task, and to learn new tasks more efficiently.

Progress in areas like transfer learning and meta-learning exemplify this. Transfer learning allows an AI system trained on one task to apply its knowledge to a similar task, reducing the amount of data and time needed for training. Meta-learning, on the other hand, involves AI systems learning the process of learning itself. This could potentially allow them to adapt to new tasks with minimal human intervention, a significant step towards AGI.

Complementing the advancements in machine learning, insights from cognitive science and neuroscience provide valuable context for the development of AGI. By exploring and attempting to replicate the mechanisms of human and animal cognition, researchers can potentially imbue AI systems with a broader, more flexible form of intelligence. This includes understanding how humans process information, make decisions, and adapt to new situations.

Neuroscience, in particular, offers intriguing possibilities. Biological brains, after all, are the only existing proof that general intelligence is possible. By understanding how neural circuits lead to complex behaviors and learning processes, researchers can gain insights into how to build similar capabilities into AI systems.

Foundational research in these and other areas is the bedrock of progress towards AGI. The journey to AGI isn't merely about improving computational power or refining existing algorithms, but also about expanding our understanding of what intelligence truly entails. It requires continuous research and discovery, weaving together threads from multiple disciplines, to create a tapestry that represents the broad and dynamic nature of intelligence. The road to AGI is both complex and exciting, as each research breakthrough brings us one step closer to achieving this profound technological milestone.

Exploration of New Models and Approaches: *Charting Uncharted Territories in AI*

While deep learning has been instrumental in propelling the current wave of AI advancements, it is not without its constraints. Some of its limitations include data and compute intensity, inability to generalize from limited examples, and the lack of interpretability or transparency in decision making. Hence, the pursuit of more versatile and efficient AI architectures has led researchers to explore a diverse array of models and methodologies.

One notable direction in this pursuit is neuro-symbolic AI. This approach aims to bring together the best of both worlds: the learning prowess of neural networks and the logical reasoning capacities of symbolic systems. Neural networks, akin to the human brain, excel at learning from data and dealing with uncertainty. Symbolic systems, on the other hand, shine in handling abstract concepts, complex relationships, and high-level reasoning. Combining these complementary strengths could potentially yield AI systems that are both learnable and interpretable, capable of understanding and explaining their decisions in human-understandable terms.

Parallel to this, there's an increasing interest in more biologically inspired models of intelligence, such as neuromorphic engineering. This discipline focuses on developing electronic systems designed to mimic the neuro-biological architecture present in the nervous system. The goal is to create more efficient AI systems that can process information similarly to how neurons and synapses function, which could potentially open doors to real-time, low-power AI applications.

Additionally, researchers are delving into intriguing concepts like artificial life and evolutionary algorithms. Artificial life studies systems related to life, its processes, and its evolution, through the use of simulations with the goal of gaining a deeper understanding of the complex behaviors of living organisms. On the other hand, evolutionary algorithms draw inspiration from the principles of natural selection and evolution, using these principles to solve complex optimization problems that traditional AI might struggle with.

The exploration of new models and approaches is an indispensable part of AI research. It's through this iterative process of trial and discovery that we continually push the boundaries of what AI can achieve. Whether it's neuro-symbolic AI, neuromorphic engineering, or evolutionary algorithms, each new approach contributes to our growing knowledge base, diversifying our AI toolbox, and ultimately, inching us closer to the elusive goal of creating truly intelligent machines.

The path towards AGI is likely to involve gradual, incremental progress rather than sudden breakthroughs. We'll likely see AI systems gradually expand their capabilities, taking on more complex tasks and becoming better at learning from small amounts of data, reasoning about the world, and adapting to new situations.

AI Safety and Ethics: Navigating the Crossroads of Technology and Humanity

As we venture further into the territory of AGI, considerations of safety and ethics grow exponentially in importance. The advent of AGI represents a leap from technology that can perform specific tasks to technology that can think, learn, and potentially make decisions autonomously. Given this shift, it's paramount to ensure that AGI operates in a manner that is beneficial to humanity and is consistent with our shared values.

One of the core challenges in this endeavor is the problem of AI alignment. The goal of AI alignment is to design AGI systems whose objectives harmoniously align with human values and interests. This alignment is far from trivial, as it requires a nuanced understanding of complex human values and their potential translation into computational goals. Moreover, we need to guard against 'value drift' - the risk that an AGI system might deviate from its original intended values as it learns and evolves.

Another crucial aspect is interpretability, often also referred to as explainability. As AGI systems grow more complex, it will be critical to comprehend why they make certain decisions, particularly in high-stakes domains like healthcare, finance, or autonomous driving. Achieving interpretability is no easy task, given the often 'black-box' nature of advanced AI systems, but it's an essential one for maintaining trust and accountability in AGI.

Robustness, the ability for AGI to behave reliably and predictably under a wide range of conditions, is the third pillar of AI safety. Robust systems need to be resistant to adversarial attacks and able to handle unexpected scenarios or inputs without failing or behaving undesirably. This includes maintaining alignment with human values even in novel or extreme situations that the system wasn't specifically trained for.

In parallel with these technical aspects of AI safety, the ethical implications of AGI must also be thoroughly explored. This includes, but is not limited to, the potential social, economic, and political impacts of AGI, its governance, and the question of AGI rights and responsibilities.

The challenge of integrating safety and ethics into AGI is significant and multidimensional. It necessitates a multidisciplinary approach, bringing together expertise from AI, philosophy, social sciences, law, and more. It also requires active engagement with diverse stakeholders, including the public, to ensure a broad consensus on what beneficial and ethical AGI looks like. While the road to AGI safety and ethics is complex, it's a journey we must undertake with utmost commitment, for it's at the intersection of technology and humanity that our future with AGI will be shaped.

While the timeline for achieving AGI remains uncertain, the journey towards it is likely to yield significant technological advances and transformative applications. It's a path that requires careful navigation, balancing the pursuit of technological advancement with attention to safety, ethical considerations, and societal impact.

AI Ethics and Regulation

As AI becomes more pervasive, issues surrounding ethics and regulation are gaining urgency. AI systems, though highly efficient, are not immune to biases, errors, or misuse, and their decisions can have significant societal and personal impacts. Therefore, establishing ethical guidelines and regulatory measures is vital to ensure fairness, privacy, accountability, and transparency.

Data Privacy: Protecting Our Digital Footprints

As AI systems continue to evolve, they become increasingly reliant on vast quantities of data for learning and decision-making, which inevitably raises pivotal concerns surrounding privacy. Every click, swipe, and interaction contributes to the data trail we leave behind, a digital footprint that AI systems harness to generate insights and predictions about our behavior.

From targeted advertisements to personalized recommendations, AI's ability to parse through and derive meaning from these data trails can be a double-edged sword. While it can enhance convenience and personalization, it also poses serious risks to individual privacy. Unauthorized access, data breaches, or misuse of such data can have profound personal and societal consequences, intensifying the need for robust data privacy measures.

In response to this challenge, comprehensive data protection regulations such as the General Data Protection Regulation (GDPR) in the European Union have been established. These regulations are designed to safeguard individuals' privacy rights, offering protection against data breaches, and ensuring that personal data are processed and stored securely. They also aim to give individuals more control over their data, including the right to know what data are collected, how they are used, and the ability to delete their data.

However, as technology continues to advance, novel challenges surface that test the boundaries of existing regulations. For instance, the advent of facial recognition and other biometric data usage have raised new privacy concerns that aren't fully addressed by existing legislation. Likewise, the growth of health-tracking applications and wearable technology has led to an explosion of sensitive health data that are potentially vulnerable to misuse.

Thus, the dialogue surrounding data privacy is a dynamic and evolving one. Policymakers, technology companies, and society at large will need to continue adapting to these changes and challenges. By crafting informed regulations, implementing robust data protection measures, and fostering a culture of privacy, we can ensure that the development and application of AI technologies are guided by respect for individual privacy.

In the era of AI, privacy should not be a trade-off for innovation. Instead, privacy should serve as a guiding principle, a pillar upon which AI systems are built, ensuring that technological progress does not come at the cost of our fundamental rights.

Algorithmic Bias: *An Unseen Influence in AI Decision-Making*

As AI technologies become more entwined with our daily lives, one of the key ethical concerns that surfaces is that of algorithmic bias. These biases can subtly creep into AI systems, often unbeknownst to the designers, causing the systems to unwittingly perpetuate and amplify societal prejudices.

The root of this problem often lies in the data used to train AI systems. These systems learn from historical data, which captures past decisions, actions, and outcomes. However, if this data contains biases, the AI systems can inadvertently learn and perpetuate these biases. For example, if a machine learning model is trained on hiring data from a company that has historically favored certain demographics over others, the resulting AI could reflect these same prejudices, unfairly disadvantaging certain groups of applicants.

Algorithmic bias can manifest in various high-stake domains, including hiring, lending, law enforcement, and healthcare, leading to unjust outcomes. Its influence can range from subtle to significant, and the harm it can cause — to individuals, communities, and society at large — cannot be overstated.

Addressing algorithmic bias is a complex issue that requires a multi-faceted approach. It involves not only the technical challenge of improving the fairness of AI algorithms but also the broader societal challenge of ensuring that the data used to train these algorithms are representative and unbiased.

On the technical front, researchers are developing methods to make AI models more fair and less prone to bias. This includes techniques for de-biasing data, implementing fairness constraints in AI algorithms, and developing models that can account for bias in their inputs.

On the societal front, addressing algorithmic bias requires greater awareness and representation. It involves including diverse voices in AI development and decision-making processes to ensure the systems we build reflect a broad range of perspectives and experiences. It also means striving for more transparency in AI systems, so that any biases that do arise can be identified and addressed.

Addressing algorithmic bias is not just a technical challenge, but a deeply human one. It involves grappling with societal prejudices that have long existed in our world. However, in doing so, we have the opportunity to not only build fairer, more equitable AI systems, but also to contribute to broader societal efforts towards equality and justice.

Transparency and Accountability: *Unveiling the Black Box*

With the increasing complexity and sophistication of AI systems, one of the growing concerns among researchers, policymakers, and the public alike is the issue of transparency and accountability. The opacity of decision-making processes in AI, often referred to as the "black box" problem, can make it extremely challenging to comprehend why certain decisions are made by these systems.

This lack of transparency is not just a theoretical issue; it has practical implications. For instance, if an AI system denies a loan application, makes a medical diagnosis, or selects an individual for additional scrutiny by law enforcement, it is crucial to understand why it made such a decision. This understanding is necessary for evaluating the decision's fairness, for holding the right parties accountable if something goes wrong, and for refining the system to make better decisions in the future.

Moreover, the "black box" problem can hinder trust in AI systems. If people do not understand how an AI system is making decisions, they may be reluctant to adopt or accept it, particularly in high-stakes domains like healthcare, finance, or justice.

Addressing these challenges involves concerted efforts on several fronts. On the research front, there is growing interest in the field of explainable AI (XAI), which aims to develop AI systems whose actions can be readily understood by human users. XAI techniques can make it easier to inspect, debug, and understand the decisions of AI systems.

On the regulatory front, efforts are underway to establish standards and regulations that promote transparency in AI systems and hold developers accountable for their AI's actions. For example, the European Union's General Data Protection Regulation (GDPR) has provisions related to algorithmic decision-making, including a "right to explanation" for decisions made by automated systems.

Transparency also extends to the datasets used in training AI systems. Openness about the source and nature of training data can help identify potential biases or shortcomings in the data that could influence the AI's decisions.

Promoting transparency and accountability in AI is a complex, ongoing challenge that will require collaboration between researchers, policymakers, tech companies, and the public. However, the goal is clear: to create AI systems that are not just intelligent and efficient, but also trustworthy, fair, and aligned with human values.

Job Displacement: *Automation's Double-Edged Sword*

One of the most widely discussed implications of AI advancement is the potential displacement of jobs due to automation. As AI systems become more competent and versatile, they are expected to take on a broad array of tasks that were previously the domain of humans, leading to significant changes in the job market and potentially major economic and social disruptions.

AI-driven automation is a double-edged sword. On one hand, it promises significant productivity gains, as tasks can be performed more efficiently, accurately, and at a scale beyond human capabilities. On the other hand, the displacement of jobs by machines raises serious concerns about job losses and income inequality.

While AI is poised to create new jobs and industries, just as past technological revolutions have, there's a caveat: the skills required for these emerging jobs may not align with those possessed by displaced workers. For instance, jobs in data science or AI ethics may grow, but these roles typically require specialized training that displaced factory or transportation workers may not have.

Moreover, the transition could be particularly challenging for vulnerable populations, including older workers, those with less education, and workers in certain sectors that are particularly susceptible to automation, like manufacturing and transportation. If not managed carefully, AI-driven job displacement could exacerbate social and economic inequality.

Policymakers, educators, and businesses will need to take proactive steps to navigate this transition. Re-skilling and up-skilling initiatives will be crucial, ensuring that workers can acquire the skills needed for the jobs of the future. Lifelong learning may become the norm, with individuals continually updating their skills in response to evolving technological landscapes.

At the same time, safety nets for those affected by job displacement will need to be considered. This could include expanded unemployment benefits, wage insurance, or potentially even concepts like a universal basic income. Meanwhile, companies that heavily utilize AI could be encouraged or required to invest in training programs for displaced workers.

The challenge of job displacement due to AI-driven automation is significant but not insurmountable. With foresight, planning, and a commitment to equitable outcomes, it is possible to harness the benefits of AI while minimizing the negative impacts on workers and society.

AI Safety: Precautions and Preventions for Advanced Intelligence

As AI systems grow in capability and complexity, a paramount concern that arises is AI safety. This term encompasses a broad set of considerations related to the design, deployment, and regulation of AI systems to prevent harm to humans and society at large. Ensuring the safety of AI systems is a multifaceted task that encompasses several aspects.

Firstly, we need robustness in AI systems. This means that AI systems must perform reliably, even in unpredictable or novel situations. AI models should generalize well, not just perform accurately on their training data, but also on new, unseen data. They should also be resistant to adversarial attacks, where slight, carefully crafted modifications to input can cause AI systems to behave erratically or make errors.

Secondly, there is the issue of AI alignment. This involves designing AI systems whose goals and decisions align with human values and intentions. AI systems, especially potential future AGI, need to understand and respect the values of the human society in which they operate, even as they learn and adapt to new situations. This is a significant challenge that researchers in the field of AI ethics and safety are actively tackling.

Furthermore, the concept of AI safety extends to include the prevention of the malicious use of AI. As AI becomes more powerful, the potential for its misuse also grows. We can already see examples of this with deepfakes and automated cyberattacks. As technology advances, we may see new forms of AI-driven crime or warfare, which could have significant consequences.

Lastly, safety concerns must be balanced against other considerations, such as privacy and usability. For instance, while it might be possible to improve the safety of an AI system by collecting more data to train it, this could infringe on users' privacy.

Addressing these safety considerations requires a concerted effort from researchers, engineers, policymakers, and society at large. AI developers have a responsibility to prioritize safety and robustness in their design and deployment of AI systems. Policymakers need to understand the implications of AI and create appropriate regulations. Society, in general, needs to engage in a dialogue about what we want from AI and how to navigate the potential risks and rewards.

Indeed, the challenge of AI safety is as complex as the technology itself. However, with proactive research and regulation, we can guide the development of AI towards outcomes that are beneficial and safe for all of humanity.

Global Cooperation: The Key to Ethical AI governance

As we navigate the future of AI, we increasingly understand that its potential benefits and challenges extend beyond individual borders. AI is fundamentally a global technology, one that has implications for societies worldwide. It's in this context that the need for international cooperation in AI governance becomes especially apparent.

Addressing the ethical, societal, and regulatory challenges presented by AI isn't a task that any one country can tackle alone. The algorithms developed in one part of the world can quickly spread across the globe through digital platforms. Similarly, the impacts of AI, such as job displacement due to automation, affect the global workforce. Hence, the development and use of AI are issues of international concern that demand global responses.

For one, international cooperation is crucial to establish universal norms and standards for AI. These could address a wide array of topics, from the technical aspects of AI safety and transparency to societal impacts such as privacy protection and algorithmic fairness. Such global standards would help to ensure that all AI systems, regardless of where they're developed or deployed, uphold certain minimum ethical and safety criteria.

In addition, international collaboration can play a crucial role in sharing best practices and facilitating dialogue between different stakeholders. Policymakers, researchers, industry professionals, civil society groups, and the public all have important perspectives on AI's future. International forums can provide a platform for these diverse voices to be heard, fostering a more inclusive and nuanced global conversation about AI.

Moreover, international cooperation is vital for addressing the geopolitical implications of AI. As AI becomes a key factor in economic and military power, there's a risk of a competitive race in AI development that could neglect safety and ethical considerations. International agreements and cooperation can help to prevent such a scenario, encouraging a collaborative rather than competitive approach to AI development.

Nonetheless, fostering such global cooperation on AI isn't an easy task. It involves reconciling different cultural attitudes towards technology, navigating international power dynamics, and building consensus on complex and often contentious issues. Yet, despite these challenges, the importance of global cooperation on AI governance cannot be overstated.

Ultimately, the future of AI is a matter of global concern that requires global action. Through international cooperation, we can collectively shape the trajectory of AI, ensuring that its benefits are shared broadly, its risks are managed effectively, and its development aligns with the broader interests of humanity.

These issues highlight that the development and deployment of AI must be accompanied by thoughtful considerations of their ethical, societal, and legal implications. As we continue to advance AI technology, we must also strive to guide its development in a way that aligns with our values and benefits all members of society.

Human-AI Collaboration

As we look toward the future of AI, one of the most promising areas is the potential for collaboration between humans and AI systems. Rather than replacing human abilities, AI can augment and enhance them, resulting in a synergy that achieves more than either could alone.

Cognitive Collaboration*: Harmonizing AI and Human Abilities*

Artificial Intelligence and human intelligence make for a potent partnership, one that brings together the unique capabilities of both entities. AI systems excel at swiftly processing vast volumes of data, identifying patterns, and drawing insights from complex data sets. They can execute tasks with an accuracy and efficiency that far exceed human capabilities, particularly when dealing with significant quantities of information.

Humans, on the other hand, shine in areas that require common sense, comprehensive contextual understanding, creativity, and emotional intelligence. These are facets where current AI systems typically struggle. By aligning the strengths of AI and human intelligence, we can achieve outcomes that neither could attain independently, leading to a new era of cognitive collaboration.

Consider the healthcare sector, a prime example of this symbiosis. AI systems can analyze medical images or genomic data with impressive precision, identifying potential issues that might evade the human eye. However, the final decisions still rest with medical professionals who bring their years of training, intuition, and experience to bear. This human-AI collaboration leads to more accurate diagnoses and, consequently, more effective treatment plans.

Similarly, in the realm of scientific research, AI systems can digest vast quantities of scientific literature, isolating relevant information and insights. This ability allows scientists to focus their efforts on innovation and problem-solving, thereby accelerating the pace of scientific discovery.

Another promising arena for human-AI collaboration lies in the realm of emotional intelligence, an area traditionally dominated by humans. Emerging AI systems are beginning to understand and respond to human emotions, which could foster more intuitive and empathetic user interfaces. For instance, AI-powered mental health applications can provide immediate, round-the-clock support, effectively triaging mental health needs. Meanwhile, human therapists can focus on providing more complex, in-depth counseling sessions.

In essence, cognitive collaboration reflects a future where AI and human intelligence are not pitted against each other but are instead seen as complementary forces. By integrating the processing prowess of AI with the nuanced, emotional, and creative capacity of humans, we can unlock new levels of productivity, innovation, and understanding.

Creativity and AI: *The Symphony of Artistic Innovation*

The realm of creativity, long considered an exclusive bastion of human originality, is experiencing an influx of AI-driven innovation. The intersection of creativity and AI is blurring the lines between human ingenuity and machine precision, providing artists across various disciplines with novel tools and techniques to enhance their work.

AI is becoming more than a tool for creative minds; it's evolving into a collaborative partner. Artists, musicians, writers, and designers now explore creative landscapes alongside AI, crafting new and unexpected forms of art and expression that push the boundaries of traditional creative norms. This partnership yields creations that are not just human- or AI-made, but a fusion of both, leading to a unique artistic interplay between man and machine.

As we venture further into the future, the dynamics of the human-AI relationship are set to evolve. The narrative is not just about humans employing AI tools to augment their creativity, but about fostering an environment of mutual learning and inspiration between humans and AI.

Consider co-designing, an approach wherein humans and AI work collaboratively on a design task. Here, AI can suggest innovative design solutions based on its ability to analyze vast amounts of data, while humans refine these solutions using their contextual understanding and creative instincts. This symbiotic process can make the design workflow more efficient, productive, and innovative.

Similarly, in the context of co-learning, AI has the potential to revolutionize the educational landscape. AI systems can personalize educational content, adapting to the unique learning style and pace of each individual. This level of customization can significantly enhance the learning experience, making education more effective and engaging. Meanwhile, teachers continue to provide the human touch – offering guidance, motivation, and empathy – essential elements in the learning journey that AI is yet to replicate.

The fusion of creativity and AI embodies an exciting evolution in the way we perceive and engage with technology. As AI continues to advance, the creative possibilities are only set to expand, opening doors to unexplored artistic landscapes and learning opportunities.

Ethical and Social Considerations in Human-AI Collaboration

As we march towards an era characterized by deepened human-AI collaboration, we are presented with a unique set of ethical and societal considerations. This emerging collaborative paradigm amplifies the necessity to address critical issues such as respect for human autonomy, privacy, job displacement, and the digital divide.

The infusion of AI into our lives signifies a profound shift in our interaction with technology. It entails not merely the employment of AI tools, but the cultivation of a cooperative, symbiotic relationship where humans and AI learn from each other, evolving together. The result of such a relationship is a synergistic whole that is greater than the sum of its parts.

The prospect of AI systems working alongside humans underscores the need to ensure AI respects human autonomy. In this cooperative framework, AI should be designed to enhance human decision-making, not override it. It should offer insights and assistance while still leaving room for human oversight and final judgement.

The role of AI in our personal and professional lives also brings privacy and security to the forefront. As AI systems handle increasingly sensitive information, it is paramount to implement robust measures to protect data privacy and ensure secure interactions.

The issue of job displacement, already a concern in the context of AI automation, takes on new dimensions in the context of human-AI collaboration. While AI is likely to enhance human capabilities and improve efficiency, some job roles may change significantly or become obsolete. Preparing the workforce for these changes, through reskilling initiatives and policy support, will be essential.

Furthermore, the risk of a widened digital divide looms large. As AI becomes increasingly embedded in our lives, it is crucial to ensure that access to AI and its benefits are equitably distributed, preventing a scenario where only a privileged few can benefit from these advancements.

At the heart of these considerations is a vision of AI as a collaborator that augments human abilities and enriches our lives, rather than a competitor that threatens to replace us. As we deepen our exploration of AI, maintaining this vision requires conscious effort and vigilance.

The potential of this human-AI collaborative future presents a tableau where AI is not merely a tool, but an integral component of our societal fabric. As we delve further into this topic, we will navigate the landscape of opportunities and challenges, and chart a course towards a future where human and AI thrive in harmony.

Regulation and Oversight of AI: *A Necessity, Not an Option*
The rising prominence of AI in our lives necessitates effective regulation. The inherent risks and ethical challenges posed by AI, encompassing privacy infringement, algorithmic bias, and misuse, make regulatory oversight indispensable. While AI offers numerous advantages, such gains should never compromise our safety, privacy, or fairness.

Regulation serves a dual purpose - mitigating these risks while fostering innovation. Striking this delicate balance is crucial, as over-regulation could hinder progress and diminish AI's potential positive impacts. Moreover, regulations should not merely be reactive but should proactively steer AI development and usage to resonate with societal values and norms.

Regulating AI raises questions of jurisdiction due to its global nature, as it transcends borders and impacts societies worldwide. At the local level, countries have started to establish unique AI regulatory frameworks, reflecting their cultural, societal, and ethical norms. Notably, the European Union's robust data protection laws under the General Data

Protection Regulation (GDPR) significantly influence AI systems' handling of personal data.

Conversely, the global stage necessitates international cooperation and consensus on standards. Cross-border issues, such as international data privacy and AI's role in international security, call for a concerted approach. Organizations like the United Nations have already initiated dialogues on establishing global norms for AI.

Designing an effective regulatory framework for AI calls for multidisciplinary expertise. Insights from technical experts about AI's capabilities, limitations, and future potential are invaluable. Legal experts can translate these technical understandings into effective policy and law. Meanwhile, ethicists and social scientists bring forth perspectives on societal impacts, ethical nuances, and societal norms. Engaging a diverse array of stakeholders, including the public, will help construct a comprehensive, nuanced, and fair regulatory architecture.

One of the principal challenges in AI regulation lies in its pace of technological advancement. With AI evolving rapidly and presenting new applications, capabilities, and risks, regulatory frameworks need to mirror this dynamism. Such adaptability might involve the introduction of regulatory "sandboxes" for testing and understanding new technologies before widespread implementation, or deploying "principles-based" regulation that provides broad, applicable guidelines for diverse technologies and contexts.

Undeniably, the task of regulating AI is complex and multifaceted. However, it remains a vital component in ensuring the future of AI aligns with our societal values and benefits humanity as a whole.

Chapter 5: Complementing, Not Replacing: Human Capabilities in the Age of AI

As we sail further into the age of AI, the horizon shimmers with vast potential and profound change. It's easy to be swept up by the tide of transformation, to imagine a world where artificial intelligence usurps our place, rendering human capabilities obsolete. Yet, as we'll explore in this chapter, AI is not the successor to human talent and ingenuity. Instead, it's a powerful ally, designed not to replace us, but to complement and augment our unique strengths. From the richness of human creativity to the nuance of emotional intelligence, there exist realms where we shine unrivaled. It's in the harmonious fusion of human potential and AI prowess where the most promising future lies. Let's dive in and explore this complementary partnership in the context of our evolving AI landscape.

Human Strengths in a World of AI

In the sweeping dance between humans and technology, we often marvel at the stunning steps AI can perform, from the mastery of data crunching to the flawless execution of repetitive tasks. Yet, it is in the unique cadence of human capabilities where we find the most enchanting rhythms of this partnership. Let's tune in and appreciate the music of human strengths that still echo unmatched in our increasingly AI-infused world.

Humans shine in realms where creativity, empathy, and complex decision-making hold the stage. Our capacity to empathize, to truly understand and share the feelings of others, is a trait currently unparalleled by AI. This ability allows us to form deep connections, understand subtle social cues, and navigate the complex nuances of human interaction.

Creativity, another vibrant hue in the human spectrum, is characterized by our ability to think outside the box and come up with innovative solutions. We can connect disparate ideas, draw inspiration from our surroundings, and generate novel approaches to tackle unprecedented challenges. These sparks of creative thought light up areas such as art, music, literature, and even scientific discovery, underscoring human ingenuity in the face of the unknown.

When it comes to complex decision-making, particularly in scenarios characterized by incomplete or ambiguous data, humans excel in deploying intuition and experiential wisdom. Unlike AI systems that require substantial and precise data to make decisions, humans can fill in the gaps, draw from past experiences, and make reasoned judgments even under uncertainty.

However, in acknowledging these human strengths, we must also recognize that they do not stand in opposition to AI capabilities. Rather, they complement them. The future doesn't lie in choosing between human or artificial intelligence; it's in harnessing the synergy of both. As we navigate this future, embracing our unique human abilities can help us shape a world where AI is an ally, amplifying our strengths rather than replacing them.

AI as a Tool for Augmentation

In the grand tableau of human achievement, AI should be viewed not as a usurper of our abilities, but as a powerful brush that adds vivid strokes of efficiency and precision. AI can be an essential tool to amplify and enhance human capabilities, painting a picture of the future where technology and human potential blend seamlessly.

The real magic of AI lies in its ability to automate repetitive tasks with exceptional accuracy and speed. From data entry to pattern recognition, AI can shoulder the burden of tasks that might otherwise require countless human hours. This automation doesn't render humans obsolete; instead, it frees us from the shackles of monotony and allows us to invest our time and cognitive resources in more engaging and meaningful endeavors.

AI also wields the power to sift through and interpret staggering amounts of data far beyond human capacity. It can spot patterns, extract insights, and make predictions with a level of efficiency and accuracy that is game-changing across sectors. This data-driven insight can guide our decisions, prompt new lines of inquiry, and accelerate innovation.

AI's prowess in performing complex calculations is another significant facet of augmentation. Whether it's optimizing logistics in supply chains, processing vast genomics data in healthcare, or solving intricate problems in mathematics and physics, AI can act as a turbocharged engine propelling us towards solutions at an unprecedented pace.

Yet, while AI handles these tasks, humans can engage in roles that require the unique qualities we possess. We can focus on tasks that call for empathy and personal connection, critical thinking to navigate uncharted waters, or creative problem-solving to generate innovative ideas. By delegating tasks that AI can handle effectively, we can elevate our focus to areas where we shine, resulting in a potent partnership that maximizes the strengths of both humans and AI.

In this vision of the future, AI is not a replacement, but an augmenting tool that magnifies our capabilities and potential. By embracing this perspective, we can look forward to a future that is not just about coexistence with AI but about co-evolution, where human ingenuity and artificial intelligence push the boundaries of possibility together.

Examples of AI Augmenting Human Capabilities

Various sectors are already beginning to see the tangible benefits of AI augmenting human capabilities. Let's delve into some examples.

Medicine: One of the most profound applications of AI augmentation is in the field of medicine. AI has shown great promise in analyzing medical images, such as X-rays, MRI scans, or pathology slides, with remarkable accuracy. It can process vast amounts of patient data to identify patterns, anomalies, or potential risk factors that might elude the human eye. However, while AI can provide these insights, the responsibility and skill to interpret them in the broader context of a patient's health lie with the human doctor. The physician takes into consideration the patient's medical history, present symptoms, lifestyle, and personal concerns. The AI system augments the doctor's capability, providing valuable information and recommendations, but the ultimate medical decision-making rests with the human practitioner.

Design and Engineering: AI is also making waves in the realms of design and engineering. AI-powered software can now generate design prototypes, optimize engineering solutions, or simulate the performance of a structure under various conditions. These tools allow designers and engineers to explore a multitude of ideas and configurations rapidly, reducing the time spent on repetitive calculations or modifications. However, the creative spark, the understanding of user needs, and the final decision on design or engineering solutions are human abilities that AI enhances but doesn't replace.

Education: In education, AI systems can personalize learning materials to cater to an individual student's pace, learning style, and interests. They can also provide immediate feedback, helping students understand and rectify their mistakes in real-time. However, teachers continue to play a crucial role in inspiring students, providing nuanced explanations, fostering a conducive learning environment, and imparting values and soft skills. Thus, AI acts as a valuable aid, augmenting the teacher's ability to cater to diverse student needs.

Customer Service: AI chatbots can handle routine queries, track customer behavior, and provide personalized product recommendations in customer service. They can manage multiple customer interactions simultaneously, offering 24/7 service, and freeing human customer service representatives from mundane queries. Yet, when it comes to dealing with complex complaints, empathizing with customer frustrations, or making judgement calls, human agents step in. Here, AI augments the customer service process, enhancing efficiency and personalization, but the human touch remains invaluable.

As we have seen from these diverse examples, the integration of AI into our work and lives need not be a story of replacement, but rather one of partnership. This view of AI as a powerful tool for augmentation paints an optimistic picture for the future. It's a future where AI helps us scale our abilities, tackle complex challenges, and enhance our efficiency, while we, in turn, provide the nuanced understanding, creativity, empathy, and strategic thinking that are uniquely human. As we continue to innovate and develop new AI technologies, it's crucial that we remain at the center of this narrative, using AI as a means to amplify our human potential and not as an end in itself. The richness of human experience and capability, combined with the precision and scalability of AI, has the potential to create a world of advancement, prosperity, and enhanced human achievement.

Chapter 6: Preparing for the AI Revolution

As we approach the final frontier of this explorative journey through the AI landscape, it's clear that artificial intelligence has the potential to bring about a profound revolution. From our personal lives to our workplaces, from the way we learn to the way we solve complex societal problems, AI's influence will be far-reaching and transformative. This impending revolution, much like the industrial revolutions of the past, brings with it a mix of unprecedented opportunities and challenges. Therefore, it's crucial that we prepare ourselves for this new era – not by surrendering to fear or apprehension, but by embracing the change with knowledge, understanding, and a proactive mindset. In this concluding chapter, we will delve into how we can gear ourselves towards this exciting AI-driven future, ensuring that we navigate this transformation in a manner that maximizes benefits for all and minimizes the risks and unintended consequences.

Understanding AI

First and foremost, education is key. Everyone, not just those in the tech industry, needs to understand what AI is, how it works, and its potential implications. This knowledge can demystify AI and dispel unwarranted fears and misconceptions.

As AI continues to permeate every facet of our lives, from the economy to healthcare, education to entertainment, a basic understanding of AI becomes increasingly necessary for everyone, not just for technologists or policy-makers.

AI often feels like a complex and inaccessible topic reserved for computer scientists and tech wizards. This lack of understanding can breed fear and apprehension. However, AI, at its core, is a tool created by humans. As with any tool, we can learn to understand it.

Numerous resources, both online and offline, offer the opportunity to learn about AI at a level appropriate for every background and age group. Websites offer free courses, YouTube channels dedicate themselves to breaking down AI concepts, and books demystify the fundamentals of AI for the general public. By leveraging these resources, we can start to unravel the complexity of AI.

Becoming AI literate involves understanding the basics of what AI is, how it works, its capabilities, and its limitations. For instance, it's important to understand the difference between narrow AI, which is designed to perform a specific task such as voice recognition, and general AI, which theoretically could perform any intellectual task that a human being can.

Understanding AI also involves recognizing its potential impacts on society, economy, and ethical dimensions. It means knowing how AI can be used and misused, being able to identify and prevent algorithmic bias, and being aware of privacy issues related to AI and data.

Importance in Decision Making

In this era of digital transformation, AI stands as a cornerstone, influencing everything from individual choices to global policy decisions. Therefore, an understanding of AI becomes a critical tool in our decision-making arsenal. With a working knowledge of AI, we can critically assess the veracity and context of AI-related news, and understand the implications of evolving AI regulations. It helps us navigate the complexities of the AI-centric workplace and allows us to leverage AI effectively in our day-to-day lives.

For instance, consider the workplace. As AI continues to reshape various industries, understanding its potential and limitations can guide our career decisions. It can help us identify opportunities for upskilling or reskilling, preparing us for new roles that emerge as a result of AI-driven transformations.

In our personal lives, knowledge of AI can help us make informed choices about the devices, apps, and digital services we use, and it can help us better understand and control the data we share with these platforms. Furthermore, understanding AI and its implications on privacy and security enables us to engage with digital technologies responsibly and safely.

From a societal perspective, AI literacy can enhance our participation in public discourse and policy decisions related to AI. Whether it's a community discussion about deploying AI surveillance in public spaces or a national debate on AI regulations, an understanding of AI can empower us to contribute meaningfully to these important conversations.

As we march towards a future where AI will permeate every facet of our lives, gaining proficiency in AI is not just an asset—it is a necessity. Understanding AI is the first step towards confidently and safely navigating the AI revolution and using the technology to its full potential, while mitigating its risks. After all, the ultimate goal is to ensure that AI serves as a tool for human empowerment, enriching our lives, augmenting our capabilities, and fostering societal progress.

Developing Relevant Skills

As AI becomes increasingly embedded in our daily lives and professional spheres, the development of relevant skills takes on added significance. Naturally, technical skills such as programming and data analysis are paramount for those directly engaged in designing, implementing, and managing AI systems.

However, the human element in the world of AI is irreplaceable and will continue to be highly valued. As we discussed in the previous chapter, AI cannot replicate certain human capabilities, including empathy, creativity, and critical thinking. These skills will be in even higher demand, and it is crucial to promote their cultivation within our educational systems and professional environments.

The promise of AI extends far beyond individual benefit or business profit. This technology has the potential to address some of the most formidable challenges we face as a global society, ranging from mitigating climate change to revolutionizing healthcare. It is our responsibility to harness AI for these beneficial applications, supporting organizations and initiatives that align with these objectives.

As we progress in the AI era, it is critical that the advantages brought about by this technology are shared equitably. It involves concerted efforts to eliminate biases from AI systems, promote diversity in the AI field, and ensure that the benefits of AI permeate all strata of society.

As the unfolding AI revolution changes the face of the world as we know it, it is incumbent upon us not to stand on the sidelines as mere spectators. By comprehending the dynamics of AI, nurturing pertinent skills, advocating for ethical AI use, and actively leveraging AI for the greater good, we all have a role to play in guiding this revolution towards the betterment of humanity..

Conclusion: Embracing the Future with AI

As we stand at the precipice of the AI revolution, it's only natural for feelings of exhilaration and unease to intermingle. The transformative potential of AI is immense, yet so are the challenges and ethical quandaries it poses. However, as we have journeyed through this book, it has become evident that these challenges should not provoke dread but rather demand our active engagement, comprehensive understanding, and thoughtful action.

We have come to understand that AI is a tool - a potent one at that, but a tool in our hands nonetheless. Like any tool, its utility is determined by how we wield it. AI has the capability to automate mundane tasks, decipher patterns from complex data sets, and solve problems on a scale that was hitherto unfathomable. At the same time, we need to remain cognizant of its limitations and the ethical considerations accompanying its use.

AI is here to amplify our abilities, not supplant them. As we chart our course into the future, nurturing our distinctively human capabilities—creativity, critical thinking, empathy, and the ability to navigate intricate social dynamics—is paramount. These skills, coupled with a fundamental understanding of AI and a forward-thinking approach, will empower us to effectively steer through the waves of the AI revolution.

In conclusion, we should envision AI not as an adversary, but as an ally—an ally that opens doors to enhanced productivity, problem-solving, and the enrichment of our daily lives. Admittedly, the journey ahead is peppered with challenges, and they require our thoughtful navigation. However, armed with understanding, proactive regulation, and an emphasis on human augmentation, we are well-equipped to ensure that the AI revolution is a leap forward for all of humanity.

The future of AI is not merely a predetermined path, but a journey we are actively shaping. So, let's step into this future with open minds and an embracing attitude, ready to harness the immense potential of AI while carefully managing its challenges. What awaits us is not only a world of technological marvels but also a journey of discovery, growth, and human potential like we've never seen before.

www.ingramcontent.com/pod-product-compliance
Lightning Source LLC
Chambersburg PA
CBHW070135230526
45472CB00004B/1535